How to Sell More on LinkedIn

Table of Contents

1. Who Am I?
2. Welcome to LinkedIn
3. A Few Statistics About LinkedIn
4. LinkedIn Is More Than Just Resumés
5. How LinkedIn Really Works
6. All About the New LinkedIn
7. Expanding Your Business and Becoming a Thought Leader on LinkedIn
8. Getting Started (Or Re-Started) On LinkedIn The Right Way
9. LinkedIn Profile Deep Dive
10. Marketing and Selling
11. Content Marketing on LinkedIn

Who Am I?

Thanks for picking up this book. Before we get rolling, I want you to know who you're talking to.

My name is Alfred Lakudzala and I'm a Business Development Consultant and LinkedIn crusader at Gwintern in Hampshire, England.

By day, you can bet I am on the computer pushing that LinkedIn value-added marketing message to my professional practice clients or coordinating that personalised video commercial for yet another client. Alongside all this, I will be preparing content or some blog posts and cleaning up some LinkedIn profile summary pages or even complete re-writes for busy professionals.

By night, I am typically busy chatting away either with my 14 year old son who wants to do architecture at university or my dear wife while I help her out preparing that family dinner. Once in a while I take a sneak peek at Twitter, Facebook or even an attempt at Instagram. And yes you have guessed right, I always have my mobile device by my side to review messages, updates and comments as well as to acknowledge LinkedIn connections and responding to connect requests. Oh yes I do acknowledge every connection with a personal message.

On a more glamorous scale, I lead and manage a diverse team of specialists, each passionate about technologies and business solutions that add value to and enhance the operations of successful Professional Practice and Consultancy Offices. We are all committed to helping professional practices embrace easier, more modern and cost-effective methods of lead generation and conversion. For our Clients, we scour the web identifying and sourcing tried and tested methods that have been specifically adapted to modern lifestyle advancements and social developments within our Clients' target audiences.

From enabling lawyers reach prospects with personalised messages that capture the attention of individuals, to empowering plumbers to send unique and compelling videos that speak directly to clients using their name. And yes anything in between, is covered.

You are welcome to look me up and connect on LinkedIn

Welcome to LinkedIn!

If you're not savvy about LinkedIn, you're really missing out. Not only is LinkedIn THE largest social media site for working professionals, it's one of the largest social media sites…period. In this book, I'm going to show you exactly how LinkedIn can work for you and your business. Doesn't matter what you sell, either. Doesn't matter if you're running a freelance business, or you're a vice-president of a major corporation. LinkedIn means sales and sales means money for you and your business. Follow my advice in this book, and you'll get a lot more of each.

Also, I help business owners, managers, and professionals just like you use LinkedIn for business. If you would like more information about the services I can offer you, please take a look at my contact information below. Feel free to reach out to me for a quick, exploratory discovery web chat.

Alfred Lakudzala

Contact Info:

 alfred-lakudzala-23ab421b

 alfred@gwintern.com

 GWINTERN1

A Few Statistics About LinkedIn

There are currently 476 million LinkedIn users. Let me put that into perspective for you. According to Wikipedia, there are 7.5 billion people in the world. Divide 7.5 billion by 476 million, and you'll find that one out of every 16 people on the planet is on LinkedIn. Did you hear me? If so, that statistic should shock you. These are real accounts too. Real people. Unlike some other social media platforms, Twitter for instance, that are rife with automated accounts run by bots and computer programs (not real people), the accounts on LinkedIn belong to real live human beings. Not that you ever would need to, but in theory you can reach one out of every 16 people on this planet through LinkedIn. It gets better too. LinkedIn accounts belong to business people. People who are potentially interested in buying your product or service. The bottom line is this. You can get in front of decision makers on LinkedIn for virtually any type of product or service with virtually any company in the world. As a business person, this should excite you to no end.

Let me tell you a few more statistics that will keep you awake at night.

LinkedIn Is Huge!

Of the 476 million LinkedIn users, 40% of LinkedIn users log in daily. 40% of 476 million is 190 million. That means that 190 million people, worldwide, log into LinkedIn daily.

Here's what that means...if you reach out to someone, really doesn't matter who, within just a few weeks they'll see your InMail or your message. And, there's a strong likelihood they'll want to build a relationship with you online—a relationship that might potentially lead to a sale, or more.

Here's another pregnant statistic. 133 million of LinkedIn users is in the United States. If you sell in the US, or want to sell TO the US, you can get in front of 133 million American business people using LinkedIn. There are only about 350 million Americans. So, these 133 million are going to represent virtually every business person in the US. What a gold mine!

After reading that, you might think that LinkedIn is dominated by the United States. Well...yes and no. LinkedIn is currently available in 24 different languages. Virtually any language spoken in a country you would want to do business in is represented on LinkedIn.

I know this is exciting, and that's why I wrote this book. Let's look at LinkedIn in a different way, and we'll see even more exciting news.

Used right, you really don't need any other prospecting resource other than LinkedIn. Or, look at it this way. Looking for angel investors? They're all on LinkedIn. Looking for customers/clients? They're all on LinkedIn.

All you have to do to leverage this massive resource is learn how to use LinkedIn to reach your target market. Once you do that, the world will be your proverbial oyster, and you'll never again lack for business or business connections.

Now that I've set the stage, we're going to go deep into how LinkedIn works and how you can work it to benefit yourself and your business. I help businesses and business professionals just like you with all of this. If you need any help, please reach out to me. My contact information is available in various places throughout this book.

LinkedIn Is More Than Just Resumés

LinkedIn was started in 2002. Back in the day it was a repository for online resumés. Wow. Has it ever grown and changed! A lot of business people still think of LinkedIn as just a job resource, a great place to meet future employers and employees. Recruiters are heavy users of LinkedIn. Because of this a lot of people don't really think of LinkedIn as a place to do business and make sales. Over the years, though, LinkedIn has grown into the place, *par excellence*, to prospect for new business. Here's what is really exciting. If you know how to leverage LinkedIn, you can create an amazing amount of business fast. It doesn't really matter what you sell, either. You can sell airplanes or t-shirts, medical supplies or resort real estate. LinkedIn is the place to be to create business, sales, and more revenue for yourself and your company. It's grown way, way beyond just a place to post resumés and get a job. Done right, LinkedIn might be the only prospecting resource you'll ever need. Keep reading, because I'm going to break this whole thing down for you.

In the rest of this book, I'm going to show you exactly what you need to do to turn your LinkedIn account into a sales engine the likes of which will astound you. Buckle up! This is going to be a fun ride!

The first step of our journey together is learning exactly how LinkedIn works. Once you understand that, I'll show you step-by-step exactly what to do. (If you don't have time to do all of this yourself, let me know. Helping professionals just like you is exactly what I do for a living.)

Next stop…how LinkedIn actually works.

How LinkedIn Really Works

6 Degrees of Separation

You've heard of the idea of six degrees of separation? It's the concept that all of us on Planet Earth are six or fewer connections apart. So, between any two random people, Ethel and Jerry, worst case Ethel would know Fred, Fred would know Ricky, Ricky would know Lucy, etc.…six times…and you would work your way finally to Jerry. (Yes, I used names from The Lucy Show…and added in Jerry Seinfeld for good measure. Just keeping it fun!)

LinkedIn works the same way.

On LinkedIn, let's say I'm connected with Bob. So, we call Bob a first-tier connection. Next, let's say Bob is connected with Sam, but I'm not connected with Sam directly. Sam is a second-tier connection. And, if Sam is connected with Jane, but neither Bob nor I am connected with her, then Jane's a third-tier connection.

Why is this so important? Let me explain.

Although it's important to be directly connected with people on LinkedIn, the real power of the platform lies in your second-tier connections. Here's a good example. Let's say I was connected to only five thousand people. In general, my second-tier connections would be about a million. My third-tier connections would be several million. The number of connections grows exponentially.

The real power here lies in how LinkedIn lets me reach out to these new levels of connections.

2nd And 3rd Tier Connections

I can easily use LinkedIn search and search my 2nd tier connections. I can do so using very specific keywords. So, let's say I were selling a product or service that independent automobile dealerships might be interested in. Using LinkedIn's search feature, I would be able to find a few hundred prospects just in my 2nd tier connections. Probably more. Next, I can send these people connection requests. A good number of them will accept my connection request, which will in turn expand my network in that market niche.

The bottom line is this. If you grow your network the way I'm going to teach you in this book, you'll have the ability to target very tightly defined niches, defined both geographically and by business type. With this, you'll be able to target exactly the right businesses for your product or service. What power! Are you starting to get a feel for how powerful LinkedIn actually is? I hope so! I've been using LinkedIn for years, and I'm excited just explaining this to you.

There's more though than just being able to target the right business owners and managers. There's so much more power in this platform. Keep reading! In the next section, I'm going to cover a few of the bigger changes that have happened to LinkedIn recently…good changes.

All About the New LinkedIn

In 2016, Microsoft brought LinkedIn. Over the next six to twelve months, they rolled out some massive changes. So that you have complete, up-to-date knowledge of how LinkedIn works, including its new interface, I wanted to go over some of the more visible changes and how they might affect you.

New Newsfeed

When you log in to LinkedIn, you land on a page that has what's called the "newsfeed" running down the left-hand side. That's always been there. So, that part hasn't changed. What has changed, however, is the composition of what's in the newsfeed.

LinkedIn has modeled their new newsfeed on Facebook's newsfeed. Now, you see a combination of articles, Pulse blog posts, native ads and sponsored ads. (Again, looks a lot more like Facebook.)

The important question to understand is this. Why did LinkedIn make these changes? Well, it's pretty simple actually. Microsoft wanted to emphasize the importance of content on LinkedIn. This is huge news for business people like yourself, because this gives you a solid clue as to how you can leverage LinkedIn in the future in order to create more business for yourself and your company.

Content is now king! LinkedIn's goal is to have users not only using the platform to network, but to read and experience content. All kinds of content too. As a related side note to all of this. Content on LinkedIn is indexed by Google. This is a techy way of saying that if you create a status update, a Pulse post, or even structure your profile summary that it can be more easily found by search engines, you'll end up getting people finding your content from outside LinkedIn.

For business people, the implications of this are straight forward. In order to really leverage LinkedIn moving forward, you're going to need to be creating and posting content…a lot of content. Content that brands you and your business. Content that educates your target audience. Content that hopefully leads your readers and viewers to take the next step…get on your list, call you, make an appointment.

That's the good news.

The downside of all of this is the following: When do most business people have time to create all this content? If you're a professional sales person, running or managing a business, or a manager looking to market themselves and their company, you already have a job. You're already working sixty hours a week. When are you supposed to research and write relevant content?

Answer: You're not. You can let me do it for you. Helping professionals just like you create compelling content and posting it to LinkedIn is one of the many services I offer. My contact information is at the front of this book. Reach out to me and let's talk about this!

More and Better Analytics

Another big change that's happened since Microsoft bought LinkedIn is this. They've revamped analytics having to do with content that you create and post. Used to be that you could only see how many people viewed your profile, and according to your level of subscription who those people are, now you can get a lot more information about who's interacting with your content.

For instance, you can now see who's liked a specific piece of content, what company they are with, and even what role they're in at that company. For people like yourself who want to really leverage LinkedIn, this is a gold mine. (And, it underscores even more Microsoft and LinkedIn's commitment to good content.)

Let's say you write a blog post (or have someone write it). You post that. Several people interact with it. Now you can see who those people are and reach out to them. They already "know" you. They selected your post, your status update, to react to. Now you can reach out to them and connect, message them, perhaps even suggest an exploratory call with them. This isn't cold prospecting because the prospect has already selected you. This is warm prospecting of the best kind.

These are just two of the exciting changes Microsoft has rolled out. Let me tell you about a few more equally exciting upgrades.

New Search Capabilities

Used to be when you searched LinkedIn, you had to either search people OR search groups OR search other categories. No one really searches like that. Again, similar to search on Facebook, Microsoft combined all of these search categories. Now, with one search you can see everything that gets triggered by your search phrase.

Facebook Like Messaging

Another "Facebook like" upgrade was in LinkedIn's messaging feature. LinkedIn now has more of an instant messaging look and feel. Now, when you log in, you'll see a tab (currently at the bottom right of the screen) that you can open. When you do so, you'll see all your current messages. Used to be you had to open a separate page to see messaging. In the new message tab, you can see which messages you need to respond to. For people using LinkedIn for sales, this is a major improvement. And, it fits right in with LinkedIn's emphasis on content marketing. That connection might not be so obvious. So, let me explain.

The big reason to do content marketing on LinkedIn isn't just so that more people in the world know about you. It's not just branding. You actually want people to find your content and react to it. You'll then connect with them and message them. This turns a random visitor to your most recent post into a prospect for your business. Messaging is actually step two of a specific process that I and many LinkedIn professionals use to target prospects and land more deals.

Calendar Chatbot

Chatbots are new on the Internet scene. They're basically semi-intelligent pieces of software that mimic real humans. It hasn't rolled out yet, but soon LinkedIn is implementing a chatbot that will help you schedule appointments with people you're connected to. Basically, it looks at your calendar and the other person's calendar and finds possible times for appointments. LinkedIn's goal is to keep you in their ecosystem. That's not a bad thing either. Done right, you can get more business from LinkedIn than anywhere else online. So, personally, I'm all for this.

New Blogging Platform

The final change I want to talk about has to do with, yet again, content. (Did you figure out that LinkedIn is big on content?) There are essentially two ways to place content on LinkedIn. You can do what's called a status update. (Just type something into your newsfeed.) Or, you can create a longer blog post. Blogging is extremely important on the new LinkedIn. You can get hundreds of people looking at just one post without doing any additional marketing. That traffic just comes gratis of LinkedIn's internal workings. And, as I said above, you can see who those people are and interact with them.

Before the recent changes, you had to navigate over to a separate platform in order to post a longer blog post. Now, you can do it right from your newsfeed.

In Summary

In summary, LinkedIn's most important changes fall into two categories, content and messaging. The connection might not seem clear at first. But there's a very important connection between the two. More and better content leads to more people looking at that content. That in turn leads to more people reaching out to you, and more leads for you to reach out to. Business is built through networking and content leading into intelligent messaging is the perfect vehicle for this.

Expanding Your Business and Becoming a Thought Leader on LinkedIn

I think I've actually covered a lot of this earlier, but I want to actually put a bow on the gift, so to speak. So, let's hit this one more time.

Anyone can use LinkedIn to position themselves as a leader in their industry. You could be, but you don't have to be, the CEO of your company. You might be a new, wet behind the ears, salesperson. You could be a freelancer, middle manager, entrepreneur of a startup that's currently located in your bedroom. Doesn't matter! On LinkedIn, you can attract the attention of exactly the right people. Might be customers and clients. Might be angel investors. Might be businesses interested in mergers. It's all here on LinkedIn. And, with a little work on your part (or on my part, if you want to hire me), you can achieve virtually all your branding and marketing goals right here on this one platform.

It's done, as I've alluded to earlier, with content, fueled by messaging.

All you have to do is to get a few things squared away first before you launch a full-blown LinkedIn marketing campaign. These "things" have to do with your profile, especially your profile summary. In the next two chapters of this book, I'm going to walk you through exactly what has to happen to lay the foundation for making LinkedIn a marketing and business powerhouse for you.

Getting Started (Or Re-Started) On LinkedIn The Right Way

In the last chapter, I talked about laying the foundation for success on LinkedIn. In this chapter, I'm going to start that process, and in the next chapter we'll focus on a few, extremely important details. If you take nothing else away from this book, take away what I talk about in these two chapters.

Let's get going!

Basics First—Getting Your LinkedIn Account

I'm not going into exactly how to create a LinkedIn account. Just go to LinkedIn and they'll walk you through the process. What I do want to talk about, however, is what's needed for a complete profile. Before we get into that, though, let's define profile.

When someone finds you on LinkedIn, what they see is a page that's called your profile page. It's got a variety of parts to it. Perhaps a graphic at the top, a picture of you, and a few paragraphs about you—called a profile summary. Then there's the work experience, recommendations, and more. I'm going to get into all of this in complete detail. All of these parts of your profile are important. Some parts, however, are incredibly important. Don't worry. I'll let you know what to spend your time on and what not to spend your time on.

First, let's just list the basic parts of your LinkedIn profile page.

Important Parts of Your LinkedIn Profile

- Your picture
- Headline
- Summary
- Work experience
- Keywords (so you can be found through LinkedIn and Google)
- Recommendations
- Groups and associations

LinkedIn themselves say that to have a fully complete profile that you need the following, in addition to what I just listed.

- An industry and location
- An up-to-date current position with description
- Two past positions
- Your education
- Minimum of three skills
- At least 50 connections

Just so you know. This is the minimum. Just enough to get you started. A lot of folks end here, but that's a mistake. In this book, I'm going to show you exactly what the important parts of each of these facets above needs to be in order to turn LinkedIn into a sales machine for your business. We're "going deep"! So, take notes and do what I say, because this is going to make a massive difference in how well LinkedIn works (or doesn't work) for creating more sales and business for you.

Crafting the Perfect LinkedIn Profile

Let me say a few words about why I'm suggesting you do certain things on LinkedIn, stressing some parts of your profile and not others.

In this book, I'm talking to you about how to create a LinkedIn profile that will SELL you. We're not talking about getting a job. We're not talking about resumés. We're talking about something much more powerful. Turning LinkedIn into a sales and marketing machine for you and your business.

Look back at the statistics I quoted in the first part of this book. You can reach anyone…ANYONE…through LinkedIn, if you know how.

Here's the problem, though.

If your profile is boring, if it doesn't position you and your business correctly, if it doesn't sell you, then so what?

Big deal, right? Mr. or Ms. perfect prospect is going to glance at your LinkedIn profile and then move on. They won't connect with you. They won't accept your connection request. They'll ignore your messages. They will not do business with you because your profile is weak.

A lot of people on LinkedIn think of their profile like a job resumé or a CV. It is that when you're looking for a job. But after you have a job, leaving it like that is just a waste of cyberspace. (I'm talking to entrepreneurs, business owners and managers, sales people, and the like here. If you're not interested in using your profile to get leads, create business connection, and make sales…well then you probably bought the wrong book. LOL!)

I call your profile your "silent salesperson". It's more like a sales letter online than a resumé or a CV.

To understand this, you need to understand how LinkedIn actually works.

Let me give you a little example.

Let's say you want to connect with someone, a purchaser in a certain business. What do you do first? Well, you would search for them on LinkedIn and find their profile, which you would read either on your phone or on your computer. After reading their profile, you'd decide they were someone you wanted to connect with, so you send them a connection request.

What normally happens next is this…

That person sees that you want to connect with them. Normally, before accepting that connection request, however, they click on your name and go to your profile to find out who you are.

Right there, in that brief moment, is when your profile turns into your "silent salesperson", because this new person in your LinkedIn universe will take a brief instant and read about you. You have their attention probably for the only time ever. They're reading about you. So, your profile better tell them what they need to do to a) accept your connect request and hopefully, b) do business with you.

That right there is why the profile is key to this process of turning LinkedIn into a sales and marketing machine for your business.

Of course, I just gave you the 30,000-foot view (or if you're in the metric system the 10,000-meter view). There's so much more to know about this. Details, which we'll cover in the rest of this book.

By the way, any time you get overwhelmed and just want someone to do all this for you, reach out to me. I'm here to help.

So, with all that said, let's continue diving a little deeper into understanding how LinkedIn actually works. First, if your profile is going to be a sales and marketing machine, we need to think about what you want people to know. What I mean by this is the following…

Deciding What Information You Want People to Have

The big marketing word is positioning. You need to think about what you want a given profile reader to walk away with. What impression you want them to have of you. In marketing terms, you want to think about how you want to be positioned in their heads.

So, how DO you want to be positioned?

This stems from what your goal is for using LinkedIn. Or, to put it another way, what do you want to sell via LinkedIn?

Take that goal, the sale you want to make. Now, think about why people buy that product or service from you. Your profile needs to position you as a good source for whatever that is.

There's more. More details to talk about, and we're going to get into those next.

Getting Found in Other Ways

My last example started with you reaching out to someone. And, that does happen a lot. We also want prospects to reach out to us. This begs the question of how do they find us in the first place?

Your other marketing, your business card, your website, and any other way you tell people about yourself of course would lead to people searching for you on LinkedIn. Another very important way people might try to find you, or at least someone who offers your products or services would be through either Google or LinkedIn search.

Let's say you're a service provider, and you offer commercial insurance. You're a commercial insurance broker in Atlanta, Ga. How would someone find you online? Well, they'd go to Google or LinkedIn and type in "commercial insurance broker Atlanta Georgia", or something to that effect. Then they'd get a list of search results, and hopefully yours would be near the top so that they would click on your result and land on your profile instead of one of your competitors'.

Although you can't make this happen all the time, you can heavily influence your chances of being found by including the right words in your headline and your profile summary. I'll have more to say about this later in its own section. This chapter is more of an overview. I'm sure you can see, however, that being found through search terms could be very important for your success, and that you'll want to maximize your chances of this happening.

Next, let's talk briefly about how your profile actually brands or positions you after someone lands on the page.

The All-Important Headline

The first thing people are going to actually read about you is your headline. That shows up not only on your profile, but it shows up under your picture when they look at who has viewed their own profile. (Kind of like a Facebook ad.)

You want your headline to grab them and let them know who you are.

Headlines in general aren't used to persuade. They're used to sort. A headline in an online sales letter just divides the viewers into two groups. Those who are interested enough to read more, and those who have no interest at all.

Your headline should do the same thing.

Going along with the commercial real estate example, if someone's not in the market for commercial insurance, they're not going to be nearly as interested in you, or even in connecting with you, as someone who actually needs commercial insurance. That's perfectly fine. As marketers and sales people, we don't need tyre kickers. We need real prospects who are ready, willing, and able.

So, your headline needs to clearly state what you do. It also needs to have the right words in it so that LinkedIn's internal search engine, and even Google, can pick those up and hopefully offer your profile near the top of search results.

Like everything else, I'll go into headlines more in detail below. Right now, I want you to realise the importance of it.

Graphics That Position (And Sell) You

Log into LinkedIn and just look at someone's profile. What draws your attention? We just talked about the headline, but really the most prominent feature is their picture. Your picture needs to brand and position you. It needs to be consistent with what you sell.

Here's an example.

If you sell commercial insurance, you need to look like a gal or guy who sells commercial insurance. Not only in how you dress and your hair (and makeup, if that applies), but in the setting for the picture. Unless, you're doing something a little edgy in a marketing sense, you wouldn't want a picture of you sun bathing in a bikini on Copacabana. Right?

Now, if you were a travel agent, and let's say you sold high-end vacation plans or something, then sure. Go ahead with the sun bathing picture. You're selling the dream, right? But, not for the commercial insurance agent.

I'm sure you see the difference.

There's another graphic that you need to be aware of. That's what we call the header graphic. The big graphic across the top of your profile. Most people (as in 99%) completely miss the importance of this. And, as a consequence, they have header graphics that negatively impact their message. Don't do that! Get a header graphic that supports your branding and positioning.

What to Use (And What Not to Use) From Your Work History

As far as your work history (and other positions such as volunteer positions, internships, and contract or temporary positions), there are two important guidelines. One is to always tell the complete truth. Sure, you can show yourself in the best light. Just stay well within the truth.

The other guideline to think about is to realize that you're NOT writing your profile for yourself. You're writing it for a certain audience. If you're looking for a job, you're writing it for potential employers or recruiters. If your profile is written to further your business through smart marketing, realize that your profile should be written with business prospects in mind.

How do you want your audience to see you? All while staying well within the bounds of telling the truth, feel free to massage your work history to reflect what your audience needs to see to do business with you.

All of this leads to the single most important section on your LinkedIn profile, the profile summary. Let's discuss that next.

The All-Important Profile Summary

Later on in this book, there are several sections devoted to an in-depth dive into how to craft the perfect profile for selling and marketing. Right now, I want to make one big point.

Your profile is very much like a sales letter. It's what people look at to figure out who you are, and if they want to consider doing business with you. The heart of the profile is the profile summary. Getting your summary right, and making it sell you and/or your product or service is the key to this whole process of turning LinkedIn into a sales and marketing machine.

Again, I'm devoting a lot more space to this because it's so incredibly important. Get this right, and you might never have to prospect again. Get this wrong, and LinkedIn will be yet another waste of time. Yes, it's THAT important.

As always, if you need help, let me know.

Before we launch into this, jump into the deep end of the pool so to speak, let me wrap up by saying a quick word about free and paid accounts on LinkedIn.

A Word About Free and Paid Accounts

The exact number and cost of paid accounts on LinkedIn changes frequently. So, I'm not going to list the possibilities. There are only a few. This book is written for sales and marketing professionals. Whether you work for a big corporation or you just started a business in your living room, if you sell, this book is for you. I'm not talking about job seekers. I'm not talking about specialists like corporate recruiters. I'm only addressing this to people and businesses who want to use LinkedIn to create more revenue faster and easier than they ever dreamed possible. (Yes, entirely possible, when you know how.)

So, with that in mind, there are three basic accounts you can get, free, business, and what LinkedIn calls Sales Navigator. Without going into complete detail (because it's not necessary), let me give you the pros and cons of each.

Free Accounts

Well, for one a free account is free. Nothing wrong there. You can have a complete profile. You can connect with thousands of people. You can basically do everything you need to do, except for one big thing. You can't search a lot.

You can search some, but at some point, if you are constantly entering in searches into the search window, LinkedIn's going to politely tell you that it looks like you're using LinkedIn for commercial reasons and that you need to upgrade your account. In other words, they want money from you. Given the power of LinkedIn that's completely fair.

When you first get an account, it will be free. My suggestion is this. Use the free account to get your feet wet, then when LinkedIn decides that you've had enough of free, upgrade.

Paid Accounts

Right now, there are two upgrades to make (actually more, but I'm simplifying). You can move up to a business account or you can upgrade to Sales Navigator. The main difference between a generic business account and a free account is you won't be limited in your search volume. Once you start paying LinkedIn, you can search as much as you want. The search interface won't change. It's only pretty good. (They took the really cool stuff and put it in Sales Navigator last year.) Having said that, for many professionals who want to make sales on LinkedIn the business account is all they need.

Sales Navigator adds a ton of new options. You essentially get an integrated customer management system. You can target specific people, get reminded of when to contact them. All the stuff that you'd expect in a high-end sales management system. It's all right there embedded in LinkedIn, and if you're a professional...sales person, marketer, entrepreneur...Sales Navigator is well worth the price. Besides, right now, it's not much more per month than the business plan.

Again, my overall suggestion is this. Start with free. Get used to the platform, and then when LinkedIn decides you've had enough of free, upgrade.

What We've Covered

So far, we've covered the basics. What LinkedIn is, how it works, and basics about your profile. In the next section, I want to take a deep dive into important details about your profile. I have a lot of experience with LinkedIn, and I'd like to shorten the learning curve for you. As always, if you need help with anything, reach out to me.

LinkedIn Profile Deep Dive

So far, I've introduced several topics. In this section, I want to go deep into several topics that are extremely important when it comes to marketing yourself or your business on LinkedIn. Virtually anyone can fill in their previous work history. One of the many things I do on LinkedIn is to provide professionally written profile summaries. Very few profile summaries that I read are done right from a sales and marketing perspective. In this section, I'm going to show you exactly what's required to have a killer LinkedIn profile that will have your contacts and viewers falling all over themselves to do business with you. Let's start by going deep into your profile summary.

Why You Need a Killer Profile Summary

All parts of your LinkedIn profile are important. None is as important as the summary. As of right now, today as I'm writing this, your profile summary can contain a maximum of 2,000 characters. That's about three hundred words. Without sitting there and counting the actual words, you want to use as much of this as is allotted to you. This is your chance to tell your viewer about yourself, why they need to connect with you, and why they need to do business with you. I'll get into what's needed for a killer profile summary next. Right now, I want to make sure you completely understand why your summary is so incredibly critical to your success on LinkedIn.

It's All About Psychology

When you play the LinkedIn game right, you're doing things, taking actions, that result in you getting more connections, in more people reaching out to you, in more people messaging you, and hopefully in more prospects getting off of LinkedIn and onto the phone or actually in a physical meeting with you.

There's a certain chain of events, though, that has to happen in order for you to get in front of that new prospect. No matter how it happens, you have to get someone's attention, and they have to at some point make the decision to start or continue a relationship with you on LinkedIn, then hopefully off of LinkedIn.

Here's the critical question. How does someone decide they want to connect with you, reply to your message, or hopefully talk to you about the next steps in the sales process? Although all the steps in this process are important, the single biggest deciding point happens when the person actually takes a second and looks at your profile.

Think about your own behavior on LinkedIn. When you login and see the little red number above the "My Network" icon at the top of the LinkedIn page, what do you do? These are the new people wanting to connect with you, by the way. Well, I click on that icon every few days and scan the people who are reaching out to me. Before I accept anyone's connection, I click on their name and go to their profile page. I'll scroll through virtually everything on the page, but not through the profile summary. I actually scan that to see who the person is and what they do for a living. Only then do I accept their invite.

Same's true when someone who is in my network messages me. You don't have to be a 1st tier connection to message someone. Right now, 2nd tier connections can message. For anyone with a healthy LinkedIn account, that's a million or so people. My point is, you have no realistic possibility of always knowing who's messaging you, who that person is. So, what would you do in that instance? Of course, you would click on their name and go see their profile…and scan the profile summary to see who this person is and decide if you're going to spend any of your valuable time with them. Be assured that everyone else does this too. And, for that very reason, your profile summary is the key to this whole selling and marketing on LinkedIn thing. With that in mind, let's talk about what's needed for a killer profile summary. One that will not only brand and position you, but get you tons of customers, new clients, more business, partners, whatever it is you need.

What's Needed for A Killer Profile Summary

Okay, so I've hopefully convinced you of the primary importance of your LinkedIn profile summary. Now, let's get down to the proverbial brass tacks. Exactly what's needed for a profile summary that will properly brand you, position you, and make people want to do business with you?

I'm assuming you're representing a business, either your own or someone else's. Either way, you need to be able to communicate what you do to your readers. And, by the way, you need to be able to do this in person. A short encapsulation of what a business does is called a unique selling point. What do you do, what does your business do, and what do your products do that is distinguishable from anyone else in the market place, especially from your competitors?

So, let's open a parenthesis right here and talk about your unique selling point, or USP as it's usually called. Then, we'll get back to what needs to be in your profile summary.

Your USP

As I said above, USP stands for unique selling point. And, the basic idea is this…you, your business, your firm, your product or products should have something that distinguishes them uniquely from everything else in the market. And, normally when I consult with businesses and business people, they sort of stare at me blankly at this point, or they just spout whatever corporate hyperbole comes to their heads.

Phrases like…We're the most trusted in the business, the best, satisfaction guaranteed, won't cut it here. As a matter of fact, unless you have a patent on something, you probably don't really have a USP in the business school sense.

Let me explain.

Let's say you're a real estate agent. In the United States alone, there are over one million real estate agents. Give me the name of a city or town, no matter how small, and there are going to be at least two agents, probably more, who can do exactly the same thing. So, phrases like "most trusted," "best," etc. are just hype. They're not true and no one really believes them anyway.

The point is this. In the classical business school sense, you probably don't really have a USP. The couple who wants to sell their house can probably find several professional, fine, experienced real estate agents to do that for them in the space of fifteen minutes. The business that needs business insurance, can find many competent professionals to work with them on that within a day. Virtually no businesses are unique. (That's why we need sales people by the way. Or looked at another way, that's why you MUST be able to sell. It's because you're not unique. If you were unique, you wouldn't need a sales person.)

Here's a thought for you. If you're like 70%+ of email users, you probably have a Gmail account. There are hundreds of millions of Gmail accounts globally. I guess they all got their account from the Google salesperson, right? (I'm saying this with a smile.) Of course not. There's isn't a Google sales person for something like this. Why? Well, one of the big reasons is they're selling something that actually IS unique, and does actually have a unique selling point.

Most small, even many medium sized businesses just don't have a real USP. Yet, you need to be able to communicate to someone (in this case via your profile summary) what you do and why they might need you.

Here's how.

Crafting A Killer USP

I want you to think about this sentence.

I help _____ do (make, achieve) _____ (in some sort of superlative way), even if _____.

Now, just for the record, I didn't make this up. This is a favorite of savvy marketers.

An example of this for a commercial insurance agent would be.

I help trucking companies lower their overall insurance costs at least 20%, even if they've been rated (in some sort of negative way).

If you're in the insurance business, you can fill in that last part. I don't know the lingo.

But you get what I mean, right?

So, before we even start to write your profile summary, you need this sentence filled in. So…create this sentence for your own business, product, service.

I'm assuming you've done this. Cool.

Next Step

So, now you've got the USP. Next, we need to think a little about your target audience.

I'm assuming your goal is to sell products/services, or perhaps to make strategic partners with your LinkedIn profile. Actually, being able to communicate with those individuals, for your profile to "hit their hot buttons" would be a good idea, wouldn't it?

Here's how you can do that.

If you took any marketing courses in college, you ran into the ideas of features and benefits.

People buy products and/or services because they want to solve a problem, broadly speaking.

The reason someone buys your product, or hires you to do a service, is because through your marketing, they believe that your product or service will solve their problem. Just saying this another way, here.

With all this in mind, the next thing you want to do is this. Think about what benefits and features your product or service offers your target market.

If you're having difficulty thinking through this, let me take you through a little exercise that I do when I write someone's profile for them. (A service I offer, by the way.)

First, I list all the benefits of their product or service. Next, I play what I call the "what does that do" game.

Here's an example.

Let's say you're running a small publishing company, and you want to attract more writers. What are the benefits of signing with you?

Let's say a benefit is you'll get their book published and available to independent bookstores worldwide within six months or less.

So, I'd write that down.

"Published in six months or less"

Next, I put an arrow out to the right of that phrase like this, and then write the words "and what does that mean" or "and what does that do".

"Published in six months or less" ➜ And what does that mean?

What I'm getting at with this exercise is I'm trying to get into the heads of my target audience. The "and what does that mean" part pushes me to explore the benefit further. (Frankly, because the benefit that I wrote down is probably not really a benefit. Looked at strictly, getting published in six months or less is a feature not a benefit, because it's a cause that hopefully will lead to an outcome that the prospective client wants.) I digress, so let's get back to the exercise.

Next, I try to answer the question…"and what does that mean" or "do". Like this…

"Published in six months or less" ➔ And what does that mean? ➔ "You'll be able to see your book in a bookstore sooner, rather than later."

I generally try to ask this question a few times for each feature or benefit that I list on my initial list. This way, I get to the emotional core of what my client is offering to their clients/customers/patients. Benefits are emotional. Features are logical. Benefits are in the head of and from the point of view of the prospective buyer. Features are aspects of the product or service.

So, what I would suggest you do at this point is to list ten or so benefits/features of your product or service, then apply this exercise to each of them in order to get to the emotional core of why people might buy that product or service.

One more thought about this. I said the word "emotion". You might be thinking that your product, your service, isn't emotional at all. Let's say you sell used computer hardware. Nothing emotional there. Or is there? Yep, sure is. More revenue gained by upgrading a business's hardware, translates eventually to more profit for the owner, or just more kudos for the employee (and perhaps a raise or a promotion). Both those are emotional. Bottom line, all decisions are emotional first, backed up by logic second. So, just in case you thought you and your business was an exception. You're not, and it isn't.

So, do the exercise, and get a nice list of the benefits of buying from you or working with you, whichever is the case.

Where Do Features Actually Come In?

We just talked about figuring out the possible benefits of working with you or buying your product. What about those features though? What about your amazing turnaround time, and the lowest cost in your market area for your product, or your next generation technology. What about all of that?

In marketing and sales psychology, features are used to prove benefits. The feature is what delivers a particular benefit.

Look back at the small publishing company that will get your book to market faster (feature), so that you have the ego gratification of seeing your book in bookstores sooner (benefit). If I were writing that profile summary, I would talk about how you'll get to see your new book in more bookstores internationally at least half a year sooner than you would with more traditional (and bigger) publishers. That's alluding to the benefit. (Politely. I don't want to just call you an ego maniac.) How I'm going to do this is more of a feature. So, either at the same point in the copy of the profile summary, or a little later on, I would add in a sentence talking about our strategic relationships with independent bookstore networks across the world, and how that results in a much faster to market time. That feature (strategic relationships) delivers the benefit (ego gratification of seeing yourself in bookstores globally). Bottom line, features prove benefits. So, for all your main benefits, you need to prove them in the copy of the profile summary with a reasonable feature that makes this possible.

(I know this is a lot to take in. Let me know if you need help! My contact information is at the beginning and end of this book.)

The Final Step—The Call to Action

Did you notice what I did in that last sentence, the one in the parentheses above? It's called a "call to action", and all good sales copy includes at least one.

You must, must, must, must tell people what to do next. You must make doing business with you very easy.

If you're a commercial insurance agent, just having your website and phone number isn't nearly enough. You must tell people what their next step is.

"For a ballpark quote, just call the number below" or "just click the calendar link below and schedule a quick, 15 minute 'get to know you' appointment."

Putting the Pieces Together

At this point, we've got all the parts of a profile summary that will make people want to reach out to you, or if you've already reached out to them, it will make people want to accept your message or your connection request.

Specifically, we have your USP, your story, your benefits and features, and we have thought about a call to action.

You can now sit down a write your profile summary. It should roughly go in this order.

1. Your story
2. Your USP
3. Your benefits
4. Your features as needed
5. Your call to action

If you're doing this yourself, as opposed to hiring an expert to do it for you, spend some time here. Don't skimp on this. Remember, the profile summary is your "silent salesperson". It is what is going to make people sit up and take notice. It's going to position you and brand you in your prospects' minds. It tells them what to do next, and how to do it.

What to Do If You Can't Write Well

As Shakespeare said, "here's the rub", meaning here's where the problem is. Most people either can't write well enough to craft a really excellent profile summary, or they don't have the time to. I'm assuming you are very interested in turning LinkedIn into a marketing and sales machine for you and for your business. I've been helping people with LinkedIn for years now. This just won't work unless you have a killer profile, and you can't have a killer profile without having a really well-crafted profile summary.

Look at it this way. Would you or your company create a new product without creating excellent marketing and advertising to sell the product? Of course not. What would be the use in that? So, why are you considering doing the same…if you are considering doing the same.

Being a DIY kind of gal or guy is fine…but not here. (If you are legitimately an expert, then this doesn't apply to you. Most people aren't when it comes to copywriting.) The stakes are just too high to have a less than perfect profile and profile summary. So, my suggestion to you is this. Either contact me or please, please contact someone who's a bona fide expert and have them do it for you.

Alright. I am now down off my soap box.

Let's talk about what else you need to do that's extremely important for turning LinkedIn into the awesome sales and marketing machine that it's meant to be.

Maximizing Your Headline

Your headline appears in a lot of important places on LinkedIn. Anywhere you can see your photo, your headline will accompany it. When someone searches for you, they'll see your photo and headline. When someone searches for anything that gets triggered by your profile summary (where their search term…called a "keyword" …is found in your profile summary and LinkedIn search thinks it's worthy of showing it in search results), your photo and headline will appear together. Finally, when someone actually lands on your profile page, they'll see your photo and your headline underneath it at the top of the page, right under your banner art, if you have any.

Your headline has a dual purpose in the LinkedIn ecosystem.

1. It's the first thing people read. So, your headline must let people know who you are and what you do…hopefully, so they continue to read more about you in your profile summary.
2. It's searched by both LinkedIn's internal search engines and by Google and plays a major factor is either of these search engines deciding to show the link to your profile higher in the search results.

Crafting the right headline is super important. Let's talk about how to do just that.

How to Craft the Perfect LinkedIn Headline

The two purposes of your LinkedIn headline actually conflict with each other. What might be good for LinkedIn and Google search, might be horrible for a human being who's a potential client or customer.

Let's say you're a commercial insurance agent who specializes in trucking company insurance. The top searches in Google for that are "trucking company insurance," "trucking company insurance requirements," "trucking company insurance quotes."

Your LinkedIn headline only has 100 characters maximum. So, you can't just string all three together. Besides it would read horribly.

You could do something like "trucking company insurance requirements & quotes". That's only 47 characters right there, with the spaces in between the words. So, this would satisfy LinkedIn's space requirements, and might also be clear to LinkedIn's and Google's search algorithms that this profile is about someone who can provide insurance information about trucking. The real problem is for the human reader, for the sales person or business owner, this headline is not only dull, it's not very good marketing. There's nothing catchy about it.

There's no implied call to action. There's nothing human about it. Nothing that elicits an emotional response.

To get the emotion in the headline, you'll need to start working a benefit into it. (Look back at the benefits and features section, above, if you missed that.) What are the benefits of getting a quote? Why get insurance or even a quote from you? Why worry about insurance at all, except for the fact that it's required?

I'm not going to go through all the work to create a benefit for this. You can look back at the benefits section and do that yourself. (It would be good practice.) Let's assume, for the moment, that one good benefit is peace of mind for the business owner. Can we work the idea of peace of mind into the phrase "trucking company insurance requirements & quotes"?

Let's see.

How about something like this?

"Want More Peace of Mind? Contact Me for Trucking Company Insurance Requirements & Quotes Today!"

That's 82 characters, and it even has a call to action?

It's still not perfect, and I think given some more time we could tweak this some more. But, I'm not going to belabor the point. I'm sure you get the idea.

Your all-important headline needs to sell your product or service. It also needs to have the right keywords in it. And, finally, it needs ideally to tell the reader what to do. With just a little more work, we could turn our headline into something that easily satisfies all three criteria.

Okay, so that's all about the headline. Before I go on and talk about yet another critical part of your LinkedIn profile (your photo), let's talk a little more about keywords. You might know this, but I would be remiss if I didn't include a short discussion of the topic.

Keywords and Key Phrases

Keywords and key phrases have to do with how people find you on search engines or in social media platforms. When you go to Google and type in "accountant Chicago", Google has a complex, automated process that it uses to complete your search and give you the results in what will hopefully be a meaningful order. Meaningful meaning normally that the best matches to what you're searching for will be at the top of the results and the less meaningful will be towards the bottom of the results. Yahoo and Bing work the same way. So do all other search engines.

Inside platforms like LinkedIn, Facebook and Twitter, for instance, you have the same type of thing going on. If you open up LinkedIn and type the same thing into the search bar, you'll get various results. Now, these results obviously aren't the same as the results you get with Google. As a matter of fact, on most social media platforms, including LinkedIn, the results you get will be different from the results that someone else gets, because you're connected with different groups of people. But, the idea is the same. People get on LinkedIn and want to find someone or find people who match certain criteria. And, LinkedIn's algorithm does its best to comply and show the best results for that person's search.

The phrase you type in to the search bar is known as a keyword or keyword phrase. Our goal, of course, will be for your profile to show up more often when someone types in something that references what you do and where you live.

Let's use an example to understand this.

Let's say that you're actually an accountant from Chicago. Or even better, let's say you're a forensic accountant. Wouldn't you like for more people who type in "forensic accountant Chicago" to see your profile near the top of their searches rather than someone else's? (Assuming you want more business, right?) So, the question is this…how does LinkedIn know to serve up your profile for that particular search over let's say someone who's a different type of accountant?

It's all in how your headline and your profile summary are written. Of course, LinkedIn knows the city you live in or that your business is based in. But getting that connected with the fact that you're a forensic accountant is the trick.

Here's how we do this. You'll need to actually use the phrase "forensic accountant" in your headline and a couple of times in your profile summary. That's a start. That will tell LinkedIn's algorithm that your profile is about someone who's a forensic accountant. There's a little more to it than just this, however.

Related keywords

LinkedIn's never going to publish exactly how their algorithm for search works. If they did then everyone would be able to game the system and LinkedIn would lose control of their search results. They'd effectively be completely manipulated by the users and that wouldn't work for LinkedIn, nor would it be fair to all the other users.

It's fairly common knowledge, however, that using keywords that are similar to your main keyword phrase (linguistically) is a good thing to do. A phrase that's related to "forensic accountant" would be "forensic accounting". Using both of those phrases in your profile summary copy would work even better to help LinkedIn find you when someone does a relevant search.

There are lots of places you can put in these related keywords, by the way. They should be in the headline sure, but you also would want to look at things like descriptions of past jobs. Your related keywords should show up there too. How about schooling? If appropriate, you'd want to salt and pepper your description of what you studied in school to include these same keyword phrases.

Bottom line is this. Figure out how people are going to search for you on LinkedIn, what phrases they'll probably use. Use those phrases as much as you can in your profile summary and also in other aspects of your profile.

Next, let's look at things a little differently. Things like your photo, which as you might have guessed is of critical importance.

Your Photo Is Not Just a Picture

I've said this before, but it's worth repeating. LinkedIn is very much like a giant, virtual Chamber of Commerce meeting. Much more than that, sure, but it's at least that, right? With that all said, what's the first way you would assess someone you just met at a Chamber meeting, or at any other business meeting for that matter?

Sure, it's their appearance. How are they groomed? What are they wearing? What are their mannerisms, and even their manners, for that matter?

Your mother probably called it first impressions and it matters a lot.

I've been stressing the importance of your profile summary and your headline. And, they are extremely important. Your picture, however, at least in my view is even more important than either of these. Why? Well, it's first impressions just like your mother told you.

LinkedIn is a virtual "place", for lack of a better word, for people to connect. It's very important that we know who we're connecting with. Your profile picture shows others who you are. Not only what your face looks like, but a lot of other important information.

Are you formal or informal? Is your business persona more edgy or more conservative? One would work well for an independent, freelance graphics or web design expert, the other would be more appropriate for a corporate salesperson.

A great idea right now would be for you to go to LinkedIn and look at a few profiles paying close attention to the photos. See what you think about each. Especially see if there's a mismatch between what the person's photo looks like, what you think of them just looking at the photo, and what their headline and profile summary say. A commercial real estate agent dressed in Bermuda shorts, for instance, could possibly be a mismatch...unless he or she worked in the Virgin Islands or somewhere similar.

Here are a few more tips about your profile photo.

1. Make sure your LinkedIn profile photo actually looks like you, and within reason is approximately the same age as you. So, a photo of you twenty years ago is going to backfire.
2. This is one of my biggest pet peeves. Those "As Seen On..." graphics some folks put on their pictures. Unless you truly were legitimately interviewed (and the interview was aired) on The Today Show or a business show for something like CNN, putting these graphics on your picture makes you look cheesy at best and a complete fraud at worst. This is an ABSOLUTELY DO NOT DO type of thing! Just don't do it...it makes you look stupid!
3. Make sure you have an appropriate facial expression and also that your face takes up at least 60% of the picture. A divorce attorney probably wants to look professional, but not grinning like you've just been to the fun fair. A graphic artist might get away with the grin, but would look silly in a business suit and silk tie. As to the 60% rule, make sure people can actually see your face. And...while we're talking about it...actually look at the lens of the camera. Don't look to the side, that makes you look shifty. Look deeply into the camera lens. Make sure that the person viewing the photo will feel like you're looking directly at them.
4. I've covered what you should wear. Bottom line here, dress like you'd dress if you were going to your job.

5. Finally, make sure the background isn't busy, and what's in the background doesn't subtract from you. You don't have to take a picture in front of a white sheet. Not saying that. But don't take the picture of you from vacation with the cruise ship in the background either.
6. Finally, and this is yet another pet peeve, don't make the picture a selfie or look like a selfie. You know how you tell is someone is taking a selfie? Their body is slightly twisted towards the camera, even if their face isn't, because one of their hands is actually holding the camera. Don't do that. If you have to take your picture yourself with your phone, that's fine. Most phones nowadays can take really excellent pictures. And, most phones have a timer. Place the phone on something so that the camera is pointing towards you. Hit the button. Take your position. Put on your smile (unless you're the divorce attorney), and then wait for a few seconds until the phone takes the picture. No twisting required!

Get these things right and your photo will brand you and position you properly. This is probably the single most important thing to do in this book. Do it right!

Once Your Profile Is Done

I know it's a lot, especially the writing part for the profile summary and perhaps the online research necessary to understand what keywords to emphasize in your headline and summary. But, please take the time to do all of this. It's going to make a big difference in LinkedIn being yet another waste of time or in it actually being a huge profit and revenue center for your business.

As always, I'm here to help. Reach out to me with any questions you have, or if you've decided you need help. My contact information is at the front and back of this book.

Now that we have your profile complete, let's talk about the next step in turning LinkedIn into a sales and revenue generating machine…getting more and more people to actually visit your profile, read it, and connect with you.

Now That You've Got a Profile, Now What?

All along, I've called your profile your "silent salesperson". Let's go over how your profile comes into play to sell you to your target audience.

When you want to connect with someone, you send them a request. If they don't know you, there's a very high chance that they'll click on your name and scan your profile, at least they'll look at your photo, read your headline, and scan your summary. Right there, right at that point, your profile serves to position you and to start a larger selling process with your viewer.

Or, suppose that someone decides, for whatever reason, that they want to connect with you. Again, before you even get the connection request, they will have looked at your profile.

You can be asleep, eating breakfast, golfing, on the phone with a prospect, meeting with a potential partner, and while you're doing this, people are scoping you out on LinkedIn, seeing who you are, and deciding if they want to do business with you, or at least to start a business relationship with you of some kind.

Your profile works 24/7, when you're working and when you're not, to build your business for you.

Done right, LinkedIn can add a massive amount of business and profit to your bottom line. Getting your profile in shape is just the beginning of "doing it right".

We're almost ready to start talking about how to market yourself and your business through LinkedIn. That's the fun part, by the way. Before we do, though, let me cover one more aspect of set up…LinkedIn company pages.

LinkedIn Company Page Basics

Most people think of LinkedIn as a website of profiles of business professionals, and that's true…it is. LinkedIn does have, however, what they call company pages. Think of this as LinkedIn's version of a Facebook page. Company pages are not required for you or your business to do well with LinkedIn. If you're a business owner or manager, however, and you sell B2B (sell to businesses), you will probably want to at least create a company page. After all, they're free.

To get started with a company page, you need some graphics and also a description, much like the graphics and profile summary you used for your own profile. The only real difference is you don't list other items like work history. Also, you'll want the company description to be in 3rd person, rather than what you should have used for your own profile summary, which is 1st person. Another difference is you'll upload your company's logo, instead of a profile picture.

Once you get this sorted, you're going to want to use your company page in your marketing efforts. Here's how to get started doing that.

Marketing Your Company Page

The first thing you should do is to link to your company page from your emails, your newsletters, blogs, press releases, that sort of thing. You can put a nifty "Follow" button right on your website that visitors can use to follow your page. The button will show how many followers you have so as to encourage others to follow you.

Next, you'll want to email your employees, outsourcers and colleagues. Get them to visit your page and follow it. Encourage employees to add your company to their personal profiles. As such they'll automatically be able to like and share your content, helping spread the word virally about your business and your page.

The next step is to publish and share content. Granted, this can be a lot of work and it's exactly the type of thing I help businesses like yours with. The mileage you get out of this, however, is remarkable. Content gets liked and shared naturally on LinkedIn. It positions your business and gets more and more people knowing about it.

This, of course, leads naturally to the final step, which is sponsored content or what LinkedIn calls native ads. Native ads are articles that you pay to get preferential placement in the newsfeeds of your audience. LinkedIn provides good targeting. So, you can focus in on the right prospective group when you drive views. You don't have to have a big budget, either. You can get a lot of views with a minimal outlay of money per day.

Again, contact me if you're interested in this as a service.

Time to Start Really Marketing!

This concludes the set-up phase for both individuals and businesses on LinkedIn. You now have everything you need in place to start marketing yourself, your services, your products, or your entire business line. In the next section, I'm going to show you exactly how to do this.

Marketing and Selling

If you've done everything to this point, you're ready to start actually marketing and selling through LinkedIn. You've got your profile set up properly. Your profile summary is written so that it's your "silent salesperson". Now, you're ready to get people actually looking at that profile and reaching out to you.

Let's talk about how that's done.

The Three Phases of LinkedIn Marketing, Attract, Build, Sell

LinkedIn Marketing done right, happens in three steps. I call these steps Attract, Build, and Sell. We're already set up for the Attract step. The Build step essentially builds on the Attract step, for lack of a better phrase. And the Sell step is pretty obvious. That's where the rubber meets the road and the prospects you've created on LinkedIn actually enter whatever selling process you have in place.

The Attract step itself is broken down into a few sub-steps. You need to identify and connect with your target audience, and also grow your connections with that target audience. Simultaneously, you need to reach out to that target audience by getting recommendations from them when appropriate, and also using LinkedIn's Notifications feature to congratulate people on new jobs, tell them happy birthday, etc.

Let's look at each of these in some more detail.

Connecting with Your Target Audience

If you'll remember, in LinkedIn there are three levels of connection between people, 1st, 2nd, and 3rd. A first level (or tier) connection means that two people are directly connected. So, if I look in my LinkedIn account and see your profile, and there's a "1st" by it, it means that you and I are directly connected. Your overall goal is to grow the size of those 1st tier connections, and also to focus them in the direction of your target audience, over time.

By focus, I mean this. Not every connection needs to be your target audience, and it helps a lot for you to have more, rather than fewer 1st tier connections because that exponentially expands the number of 2nd tier and 3rd tier connections you have access to. You do, however, want a lot of your 1st tier connections to be in your target market.

So, this all unfolds in a two-step process. You need to connect with more people generally on LinkedIn. And, simultaneously, you need to connect with more people who actually are in your target market. Where people get confused is this. They think that since they're only selling commercial insurance in Des Moines, they only connect with people who might be buyers for that sort of insurance. That's NOT how LinkedIn works, though. By being so restrictive, they're not playing into LinkedIn's internal structure.

Here's what you need to do, then. Number one, you need to connect with a lot of people. Let's talk about that, then we'll talk about how to find and connect with your target audience.

Getting A Lot of Connections

First off, let's define what I mean by "a lot". The maximum number of first tier connections LinkedIn allows is 30,000. You don't have to have nearly that many. For LinkedIn to start working in your favor, for your 2nd and 3rd tier connections to be so big that you can use LinkedIn search and really drill down into a very specific target market, you need at least 1,000 1st tier connections. Minimum between 500 and 1,000.

500 is the lowest number of connections you need, for a couple of reasons. LinkedIn just won't work that well for you if you have just 100, 200, 400 or so connections. Your pool of 2nd and 3rd tier connections just isn't big enough. Also, if you'll look at the profiles of the people you're already connected with, you'll notice something interesting. Next to the person's picture, there's a small number. It might say 295, or 378, or even 500+. It will never say 978, or 2,456. The top number is capped off at 500.

Take two people. One has the maximum number of connections, 30,000. The other has just 501 connections. They're both going to say "500+" on their profiles. Now, each person will be able to see how many connections they have, but only when they log in to their account. Logged in or not, when you're looking at someone else's account, it's never going to show more than 500.

From the point of view of how others judge and perceive you on LinkedIn, this 500 cap is a great leveler. Anyone can get more than 500 connections in just a few weeks with minimal effort. And, when they achieve that, they'll look as professional as any LinkedIn rock star. We'll talk about how to build those connections in just a few, by the way. Next, I want to talk about how to find and connect with your target audience.

Finding and Connecting with Your Target Audience

In addition to just growing your connections to sufficient size (at least 1,000), you also need to start connecting with people in your target audience, or target market. After all, those are the people you're going to either sell to or get referrals from, right?

As I said, I'm going to spend quite a bit of time talking about building connections in a future section. So, I'll leave the details until then.

After you build your general connections and also build out connections that are more focused on your target market, you'll want to start getting those people to actually notice you. Just reaching out to them and asking them to connect with you is one way of doing this. A lot of those folks will look at your profile before they decide to accept your connection. They'll learn about what you do and more about who you are just doing that. There are other ways of getting more eyeballs in your profile, though. (Because that's really where the magic is. Getting people to actually read your profile and learn about you.) Let's look at these ways of stirring up the proverbial pot.

Getting Recommendations, Birthdays, Congratulating

Another collection of great strategies for getting people to actually stop and look at your profile is by using LinkedIn's Notifications feature. LinkedIn encourages online networking. By that I mean that LinkedIn actually wants you messaging with and interacting with your network, and your connections. LinkedIn knows that the more you do that the more business you get out of LinkedIn and the more likely you'll be to get one of their premium accounts, upgrade accounts, and keep your accounts for years, not just a month or two.

If you'll look across the top of your LinkedIn home page, you see an icon with the word "Notifications" right underneath it. As of today, the icon is a bell shape. Again, things change online, so the icon might change or it might be put in a different place, but you get my drift, right?

When you click on that icon, a window opens up that shows you a lot of things, like who shared your status updates. It also shows you who's having a birthday and who's having a change in their job status.

Birthdays and job or career status changes are great excuses for you to interact with people. You can click on the notification about birthdays and it will show you who's had a recent birthday. Click on each of those notifications and you'll be able to actually tell that person "Happy Birthday." LinkedIn normally prefills your message to say just that…" Happy Birthday." I like to go one better, though. Most people don't acknowledge birthdays at all, but of those who do, most use LinkedIn's prefilled notifications. I like to write my own message that's different. I do that so people realize that I'm a real person and not a piece of automated software, and also so that they know I took time to really write something. (Here's a hack I use. I write something different for the first person on the list, then copy and paste for the next people.)

So, that's birthdays. You have the same options when it comes to job status changes. If someone gets a new job, or changes positions in their old job, you can congratulate them on that. Same idea. LinkedIn pre-fills that for you, and I don't use the pre-filled text for exactly the same reasons.

This might take a while, but it's going to pay dividends. The more ways you can get people to see your name come up on LinkedIn the better off you're going to be. The more business you'll get. The more referrals you'll get. Congratulating people and happy birthdaying them are two solid ways of making this happen. Again, I actually help people just like you with prospecting activities like this on LinkedIn. We've got a whole system in place that works well to create a lot more business for you. You can certainly do this on your own, and I would encourage you to do just that. But, if you're like most busy professionals, you'll want to hire this type of thing out. Contact me, if you're interested.

Recommendations

Recommendations are like testimonials. Getting recommendations is important for your business. Having many makes you look professional. They also help other prospects understand you and what you sell. Since recommendations are a third-party validation of you and/or your products and services, they help prospects take the leap of faith necessary to get on a sales call with you and hear what you have to say about your product or service.

LinkedIn has a specific way of going about getting recommendations. The ones you receive actually show up in a specific part of your profile. Whenever you have satisfied customers and clients, or even just people who like you and are supportive of your business, I would encourage you to ask them for a recommendation using LinkedIn's process. (You can find out more about the actual steps through clicking the link under the recommendations part of your profile.)

LinkedIn Growth Hack: Chrome Extension to Capture Emails

Before we move on to talking in detail about your connections, let me tell you about a really nifty growth hack for you on LinkedIn.

There are a number of plugins for the Google Chrome browser that will help you locate business emails for LinkedIn users. My current favorite is called Saleslift Prospector. Saleslift makes it very easy to find and collect business emails from LinkedIn. It puts these emails on an exportable file. You can export them, and then use them in your marketing. I wouldn't just download emails and spam people. That's not the idea. You'd want to use this tool in an ongoing, bigger online networking campaign.

Just a thought.

Now, let's dive into the deep end of the connections pool.

Connections

It's worth repeating that the size and quality of your connections is the heart of any LinkedIn prospecting strategy. The more connections you have, in general, the faster you can build more connections. Also, the more connections, the easier you can drill down and find even more connections who actually are in your target audience. It behooves you to have lots and lots of connections. With that all said, let's talk about how to do this.

How to Find Your Target Market on LinkedIn

I alluded to this topic above, but here's where we're going to dive right down into it.

Finding your target audience presupposes that you actually know who those people are. I work with a lot of business professionals, and I'm constantly amazed at how often people don't really know what their target audience is. So, the first thing you need to really get straight is who are these people.

Let's use an example.

I've been using the commercial insurance agent all through this book, so let's continue with her.

Now, I know nothing about the commercial insurance business. So, you'll just have to go with me on this. Let's suppose it's reasonable that our commercial insurance agent specializes in B2B businesses that have revenues of between 10 and 50 million dollars a year. Again, don't know if that's reasonable, but let's go with that. Also, let's suppose that she works in a specific geographical area, of let's say 50 miles radius from her office. And, let's suppose that she works with a few specific types of businesses, warehouses, trucking companies, logistics businesses, that sort of thing.

Obviously, our insurance agent needs to start connecting with people who meet these criteria. Once she's connected, she can start reaching out to them, building a more solid relationship, and hopefully move some of these people into her sales funnel. (Get them on the phone, on a screen share appointment, in the office, however this works for her.)

So, the big question is this…how do you find these people and how do you reach out to connect with them?

There are several ways to do this.

First off is the obvious way. If you've been in business for a while, you surely know people who are either past customers/clients, potential ones, or who at least refer you to prospects. This is slightly painstaking, but it's very important. You need to just get on LinkedIn and search for those people and send them a connect request. If you can't do that, you can at least InMail them. You'll need a premium account to InMail. You get a specific number of InMail's per month with each type of premium account. I'm not going to list that here, because frankly it changes a lot and I don't want this book to be dated. Having said that, just go to your LinkedIn account. You should be able to figure out how many you have at your level of subscription pretty easily. If you go over your monthly allotment, however, it's going to cost you. Prices start at $10 per InMail and go down if you buy more. (It ain't cheap.)

Once you get connected with your past customers, clients, referral partners, etc., you'll want to keep this up as you meet new people. Get in the habit of connecting with new people that you meet in the course of your business. Get purposeful about building out your connections.

Using Search to Build New Connections

Beside just connecting with people you meet, you can use LinkedIn's own search feature to find businesses and people who are in your target market and connect with them.

Exactly what you can search with LinkedIn's search feature varies a lot with what level subscription you have. Free accounts can do some limited searching, and you can do a lot of targeting, but there's a lot more you can do with premium accounts. I've had the experience of LinkedIn eventually limiting your searches for free account. They send you a "slap on the wrist" notification saying that it looks like you're using this account for commercial purposes and that you need to upgrade. (Completely fair in my book. No reason I should get all this power for free, and LinkedIn is so important to my own business and my clients' businesses, I'm very happy to pay for a premium account.)

Here's also where the size of your 1st tier connections makes a huge difference. The more 1st tier connections you have, the more 2nd and 3rd tier connections you have access to…exponentially. What this means is the following. If you have a sizable number of 1st tier connections, then for virtually any search you can think of…business type + location…you'll find quite a few (as in a lot) of people to connect with who are 2nd tier connections.

2nd tier connections are easy to reach out to. LinkedIn makes it very easy and also free for you to send them connect requests. I suggest you don't use their generic wording. Use your own, it will make it look more personal and special and your success rate will be higher.

Of course, the more of these targeted 2nd tier connections who accept your invite to become 1st tier connections, the more 2nd tier possibilities you'll have when you do this process of searching and connecting again. People in the same industry tend to be connected with each other for business purposes. Let's say our commercial insurance agent wants to connect with trucking companies. Well, decision makers in businesses tend to be connected with each other. So, each trucking company exec that she connects with will give her a lot more potential connections that will now be 2nd tier connections for her. People she can easily reach out to and move into her fold.

Using InMails To Build New Connections

Another and potentially more expensive way of connecting with your target market is to use InMails. You get a specific number monthly for each paid subscription level. You can buy more, too, but they're expensive.

Personally, when we work with clients we use both their monthly InMails and also use their 2nd tier connections to build up their 1st tier connections.

Again, as always, let me know if I can help you with any of this.

Using Groups to Build New Connections

Another effective way to build out your connections in a specific industry is to join related LinkedIn groups and then connect with the group members. This is an excellent way to build you targeted connections. Don't worry too much about who you're reaching out to, just ask them to accept your connect request. When you connect with someone in a group, you need to reference that group. "Hi, Jim. We're in the Commercial Insurance Agents group. I'd love to be connected with you. Thanks." Something like that will work well.

A Few More Words About Connections

With everything I've told you, you should be able to build a really robust LinkedIn account within a short time. We'll learn how to actually reach out to these people and start the active prospecting process next. Right now, there are a couple more things I want to make sure you understand.

First it is about frequency. Don't take a new account and send out 200 connection requests the first day. LinkedIn is actually pretty cool about this. They won't just delete your account. They will, however, send you a "slap on the wrist" notification telling you to stop. If you ever get that from them, stop. The next step is to limit your use of your account.

With new accounts, I send out 10 connect requests per day for a while, then 20, then 30. Never more than 50. If you do this that way, you'll be completely safe.

The other thing I wanted you to know is how to export your connection. How you can do this has changed a few times over the past year. So, to make this book more general, I'm not going to give you instructions. LinkedIn has excellent support. Also, if you'll go to YouTube and search this, you'll find a zillion videos about it. Who knows? One might be from me.

Exporting your connections periodically is a good idea, mainly as a sort of backup. Also, if you want to, you can take your exported emails and put them in an autoresponder. What autoresponder to use is beyond the scope of this book. I'd use something at least at the level of Aweber, GetResponse, or Mail Chimp. If you're into automation, then sure, use ActiveCampaign or Infusionsoft.

A few more words about this exporting emails thing. LinkedIn has a certain etiquette that you should adhere to in order to be received as a professional by others. One of the big "no-no's" is spamming people. Now, the word "spam" certainly has a loose definition. With a lot of people spam means just anything they didn't want to receive at that particular moment. What I'm talking about here is sending unsolicited emails to your LinkedIn contacts outside of the LinkedIn system. It's cool to reach out to people through messaging on LinkedIn. It's not that cool to just send them an email outside the system.

I'd definitely download my emails just for backup, but I'd tread lightly when it comes to emailing them, especially with aggressive, promotional emails. Something like a nice "Hey, how are you doing?" type email that reminds them you're connected through LinkedIn is fine. But something with five paragraphs that talk all about how great your product that is sent to absolutely everyone on your LinkedIn list isn't okay.

Here's a very workable compromise. Send one or two blasts to everyone and invite them to go to a page where they can opt in to a new list that promises them something of use or interest to them. Our commercial insurance agent might offer people a PDF on how to save on their commercial insurance. This serves two purposes. One: you get people onto a permission based list. Two: you really start to find out who's interested in your offering and who's not. Thus, you start the process of separating the real prospects from the tyre kickers.

Next, we're going to talk about one of the most powerful methods of prospecting on LinkedIn. Messaging. Take notes. This is where the rubber hits the road.

Messaging

LinkedIn users can be separated into two groups. Those who know how to use LinkedIn for sales, prospecting, and business building, and those who don't. If you're in the first group, you have an extremely powerful skill that can be used to sell anything to anyone. Get this right, and you're golden.

Before we get rolling with this, I want to talk a little more about LinkedIn etiquette.

LinkedIn Etiquette

You want to come across as a professional, right? You want people to perceive you as someone whose product or service can help them solve their problems. So, it follows that conforming to LinkedIn etiquette might be a good thing to do. Makes sense?

Well, let's talk about this LinkedIn etiquette so that you make friends and not enemies there.

How to Approach People

LinkedIn is basically a virtual network meeting. Think about how you introduce yourself, or respond to someone's introduction when you're in person. If you walked into a Chamber of Commerce meeting, you wouldn't just walk up to the first person and give them a whole laundry list of your products and services, along with prices and with a lot of pushy stuff about how great you are, would you? (I really hope you're shaking your head "no" that you wouldn't do this.)

Well, if you wouldn't do this in person, why would you try to do it online? Online relationships are more, not less prone, to misunderstandings. You want to tread more, not less carefully online.

I'm sure you've been subject to very spammy messaging on LinkedIn, just as I have. You know, those huge five paragraph messages that come in unsolicited that tell you all about how great this person's next whiz-bang product or service is. All fluff, right? And, how do you react to that? Best case you ignore it. Worst case you disconnect yourself from that person, or even worse report them to LinkedIn for spamming. (Yes, you can do that.)

That's obviously not going to be the way to approach people.

You want to create a relationship BEFORE you pitch your deal. And, when you actually do tell someone about what you do, you want to do so with a light touch, inviting them to tell you that they want to know more.

Let me show you exactly how you need to approach people, get them on your side, and then get them interested in talking with you about your product or service.

How to Interest People in Your Offering and Get Them in A Sales Situation

Let's go back to using our commercial insurance agent as our example.

So I can talk about her, let's give her a name. Sally.

Sally sits down at her computer (or if she's smart, she hires someone like me to do this for her), and she starts prospecting.

She opens LinkedIn and checks her notifications. She sees that she has four connections who've just had birthdays and two job changers. Using LinkedIn's notifications, she messages each of them an appropriate message.

Next, Sally uses LinkedIn's search feature. She searches her 2nd tier connections for profiles who live in a 50-mile radius of her market area and have "warehouse" in their profiles. She gets 87 results. She bookmarks that search, starts at the top and sends a connect request to 30 of them.

Finally, Sally checks her messages and finds that seven people she's reached out to have messaged her back. She responds to them by telling them a little about herself. She'll use a variation of the following message for each.

"Hi xxx! Great to see you're doing well. Just so you know, I'm a commercial insurance agent. I handle several accounts of businesses similar to yours. Let me know if you need some more information about how I can potentially save you money with your insurance. Sally."

Short and sweet. Just a hint of salespersonship. Just gently knocking on their door and seeing if they want to chat further. Nothing pushy. Just saying "I'm here to help when you get ready".

That, my friend, is how you prospect on LinkedIn.

Most of the messages Sally answers won't respond. A few will. When those few respond, Sally goes into full salesperson mode. She takes their information and puts it into her CRM. She sends them some more information about her and her company. She asks for the appointment.

If she's smart, she'll schedule time to do this process every day. If she's really smart, she'll outsource this, or parts of it, to a professional like me. (If she does that, she'll soon have more business than she'll know what to do with.)

And, if Sally is super smart, after she attends to her outbound and inbound messages, she'll next move over to her content marketing campaign.

Content Marketing on LinkedIn

What you've learned so far will increase your revenues and sales by quite a lot. Just prospecting and messaging on LinkedIn, that is. If you want more, listen up. I'm going to reveal to you how you can have the right prospects stumbling over themselves to find you, instead of you spending your precious time to search for them. What I'm talking about here is one of the best kept secrets on LinkedIn. It's called Content Marketing, and it's how power users position themselves as experts, sell themselves, get more leads than they know what to do with and turn those leads into raving fans…all before they ever actually talk with anyone. Let's learn how to do this, because this is THE key to exploding your business on this platform.

What Is Content Marketing

Online the word "content" generally means any information that's available. Normally, we think of content as written content. So, a blog post is content. An about page is content. A sales letter is content. An email isn't really content, in this same sense, because it's not available to everyone, just the recipient of the email.

Content is purposefully used in marketing to attract people through search engines, to inform and educate and finally to sell people.

On LinkedIn, there are several ways to use content.

Your profile summary is one example. More important examples are status updates, blog posts directly on LinkedIn, and more recently native videos. Let's talk about each of these so you understand them.

Status Updates

When you login to LinkedIn you see what's called your "newsfeed". That newsfeed is a compilation of the status updates of various LinkedIn users. Now, there are over half a billion LinkedIn users, so obviously not everything makes its way into your newsfeed. Exactly what does is part of LinkedIn's newsfeed algorithm that is essentially "secret". Knowing or not knowing how the newsfeed works isn't the deal here.

Here's the deal.

A lot, as in massive numbers, of people *who aren't already connected with you*, regularly see your newsfeed. Do you see the potential in this? Just posting the right things to your newsfeed starts the process of attracting your target market to you. In online marketing-speak, this is called inbound marketing, which according to HubSpot is " a technique for drawing customers to products and services via content marketing, social media marketing and search engine optimization."

You need to be posting relevant and valuable information that positions you as an expert in your target market regularly in your status updates.

That's the good news. Here's the maybe not so good news.

For maximum effect, you need to be doing this several times a day. As in at least five times a day.

That's a lot of content to source, and a lot to post. (This, frankly, is where people just give up and call me. I do this all the time for clients just like you.)

Frequent daily status updates are the backbone of a great content marketing campaign on LinkedIn. They're not the only thing you need to do, though.

Blog Posts

You can, and should, be posting longer blog posts on LinkedIn. We used to call the part of the LinkedIn platform that handles this LinkedIn Pulse. (From a platform that LinkedIn bought a few years ago and integrated into their own platform.)

Blog posts need to be three hundred to five hundred words long. They are excellent opportunities for you to go deeper into your branding, positioning, and education of your target market. What's so cool about blog posts on LinkedIn is this…LinkedIn provides the traffic. You'll get a lot of "eyeballs" on your post all while doing no extra marketing yourself. Blog posts are an excellent way for you to attract the right market, separate yourself from your competitors, and start building a real, loyal following in your market niche.

Our friend Sally could write blog posts about several topics, explanatory topics about commercial insurance, articles about saving money with her company, articles explaining the intricacies about commercial insurance, and more. All of these types of articles would position her as a real expert and attract the right potential clients into her world.

Again, bottom line, you need to be posting blog posts on LinkedIn. This one thing will massively increase your revenue, sales, and especially profits.

Also, just as with status updates, there are pros and cons. The pros are that this flat out works. The cons are that writing takes time. Again, let me know if you need help. I can handle all your content marketing needs for you. You get the leads and the sales. I do the work.

Native Videos

Are you familiar with streamed videos on Facebook or Instagram? Right now, LinkedIn is rolling out their own version of these. They're called "native videos". And, if you're not worried about showing your face on a video, and you feel comfortable talking coherently about business topics, native videos are fabulous ways to advertise yourself, position and brand yourself, and generally to get a ton of business.

Native videos are new, and we're going to have to see how well they work on LinkedIn, but they work great on other social media platforms for marketing purposes. So, they'll probably work well here too. If you're in to this, get hip to it and try it out.

Content Marketing Summary

Content marketing is the single best thing you can do with LinkedIn for marketing purposes. If you'll combine content marketing with intelligent messaging, you're going to have a prospecting and sales machine the likes of which you've only dreamed of. Again, if you need help with any of this, let me know.

By the way, if you own a larger company and you want your employees to help you create a viral LinkedIn campaign, you'll want to learn about LinkedIn Elevate. This is a content aggregator that your employees can access and share to other social media platforms. Need to know more? Let me know.

Conclusion

We've covered so much in this short book. I hope I've convinced you that LinkedIn is the place for you to be for business building. If I can do anything to help you with your LinkedIn marketing, let me know. I have several ways I can help you, and I can tailor solutions to virtually any budget.

www.ingramcontent.com/pod-product-compliance
Lightning Source LLC
Chambersburg PA
CBHW062344220526
45469CB00008B/2834